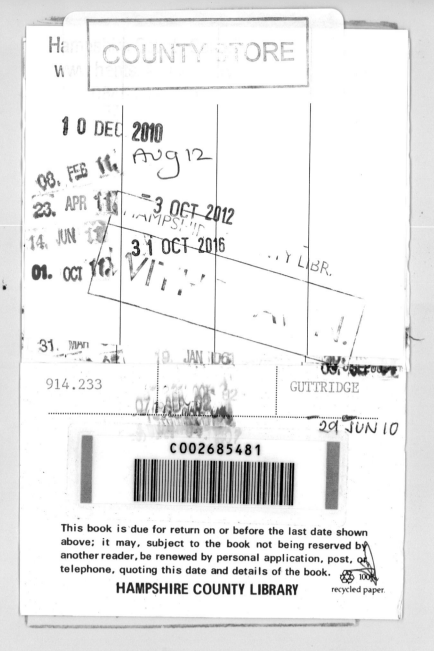

COUNTY STORE

10 DEC 2010

Aug 12

08. FEB 1

23. APR 1

-3 OCT 2012

14. JUN 1

31 OCT 2016

01. OCT 1

VIT

31. MAR

19. JAN 106

Y LIBR.

914.233

GUTTRIDGE

07. AUG 02

29 JUN 10

C002685481

This book is due for return on or before the last date shown
above; it may, subject to the book not being reserved by
another reader, be renewed by personal application, post, or
telephone, quoting this date and details of the book.

HAMPSHIRE COUNTY LIBRARY

100%
recycled paper.

D1148002

THE
LANDSCAPES
of
DORSET

THE
LANDSCAPES
of
DORSET

PHOTOGRAPHS BY
Roger Holman & Roger Lane

WORDS BY
Roger Guttridge

Ensign
PUBLICATIONS

All photographs copyright © Roger Holman and Roger Lane 1991
All text copyright © Roger Guttridge 1991
Arrangement and design copyright © Hampshire Books Ltd. 1991

All rights reserved.

No part of this publication may be reproduced, stored in a retrieval system or transmitted in any form or by any means, whether electronic, mechanical, photocopying, recording or otherwise, without the prior written permission of Ensign Publications.

HYTHE LIBRARY
NEW ROAD
HYTHE SO4 6BP
TEL: 843574

First published in 1991

by **Ensign Publications**

a division of Hampshire Books Ltd.,

2 Redcar Street

Southampton SO1 5LL

HAMPSHIRE COUNTY LIBRARY

914.
233

185455073X

C002685481

COF

ISBN 185455 073 X

Publisher: *David Graves*

Design: *Mark Smith*

Page make-up: *The Design Laboratory*

Typesetting: *The Precinct Press*

Printers: *Printer Portuguesa, Lisbon*

Repro: *MRM Graphics, Winslow*

Half-title verso: Roger Holman's award-winning photograph of Fiddleford Mill

Title page: Stone walling in Purbeck

Front cover : Looking west from Lambert's Castle above Marshwood Vale

Back cover : Chesil Beach

FOREWORD

Appearing opposite the title page is the photograph which deservedly won Roger Holman the Best of Britain award last year.

There is a translucent quality to the light which has produced one of those rare moments of photographic vision. Whilst one can almost feel the sharp frost of a bright Dorset morning, an area of warm light surrounds the mill and offers a hint of comfort. It is a picture of almost timeless quality and one that can stir the senses.

Such a reaction underlines the power of photography. Whether it be to persuade or intrigue as in advertising, or to reveal as in photo-journalism, the camera opens up a new world, even to those who at the same time often remain visually unaware themselves.

Landscape and photography are synonymous with light. Without light in all its brilliant hues and dim tones there can be no photograph, a landscape cannot be revealed.

In this book various elements have been brought together with great skill. The resulting images reveal landscapes of many very different types, captured in a variety of interesting light conditions.

These photographs can be quietly enjoyed. But they also possess a visual power beyond the printed page. A power that should persuade all of us to appreciate and preserve that which we have now for future generations.

Colmer's Hill,
west of Bridport

Sunset above
Kimmeridge

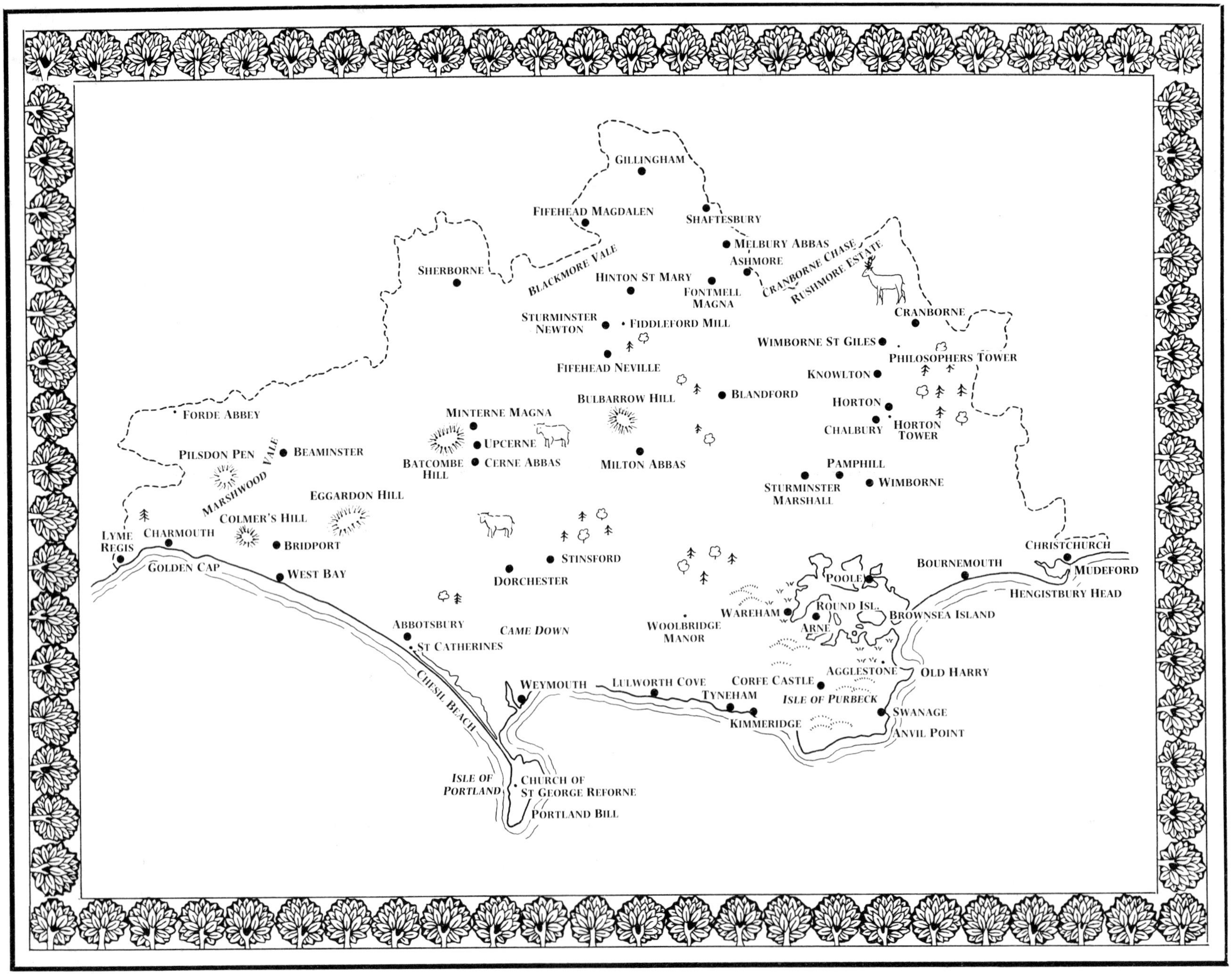

GILLINGHAM

FIFEHEAD MAGDALEN

SHAFTESBURY

MELBURY ABBAS

ASHMORE

SHERBORNE

BLACKMORE VALE

HINTON ST MARY

CRANBORNE CHASE

RUSHMORE ESTATE

FONTMELL MAGNA

CRANBORNE

STURMINSTER NEWTON

• FIDDLEFORD MILL

WIMBORNE ST GILES

PHILOSOPHERS TOWER

FIFEHEAD NEVILLE

KNOWLTON

• FORDE ABBEY

BULBARROW HILL

BLANDFORD

HORTON

CHALBURY

HORTON TOWER

MINTERNE MAGNA

PILSDON PEN

BEAMINSTER

MARSHWOOD VALE

UPCERNE

PAMPHILL

BATCOMBE HILL

CERNE ABBAS

MILTON ABBAS

STURMINSTER MARSHALL

WIMBORNE

EGGARDON HILL

COLMER'S HILL

LYME REGIS

CHARMOUTH

BRIDPORT

STINSFORD

CHRISTCHURCH

GOLDEN CAP

WEST BAY

DORCHESTER

BOURNEMOUTH

MUDEFORD

POOLE

HENGISTBURY HEAD

ABBOTSBURY

CAME DOWN

WOOLBRIDGE MANOR

WAREHAM

ROUND ISL.

BROWNSEA ISLAND

• ST CATHERINES

ARNE

CHESIL BEACH

WEYMOUTH

LULWORTH COVE

CORFE CASTLE

AGGLESTONE

OLD HARRY

TYNEHAM

Isle of Purbeck

KIMMERIDGE

SWANAGE

ANVIL POINT

ISLE OF PORTLAND

• CHURCH OF ST GEORGE REFORNE

PORTLAND BILL

Map by Sylvie Guttridge

8

CONTENTS

Sandstone cliffs and shingle at West Bay, Bridport

Thatched cottage at Fifehead Magdalen

PHOTOGRAPHIC CREDITS

The photographers Roger Holman and Roger Lane work very much as a team. In the compilation of their audio/visual presentations and in the preparation for this book they have spent many long hours discovering and revisiting the scenes portrayed in this book, each seeing them through different lenses in a figurative sense and, as the equipment review on page 24 reveals, often in a physical sense as well.

It is very difficult to distinguish between the work of these two fine photographers but with that in mind the following analysis shows the individual credits.

Roger Holman: back cover, opposite title page, pages 6, 7, 11, 15, 23, 30, 31, 35, 37, 38, 42, 43, 44, 45, 46, 47, 52, 55, 57, 58, 62, 63, 66, 67, 68, 69, 70, 74, 76, 77, 78, 79, 80, 81, 82, 83, 84, 85, 86, 87, 89, 90, 91, 92, 95

Roger Lane: front cover, title page, pages 10, 14, 18, 19, 22, 26, 27, 33, 34, 36, 39, 40, 41, 48, 49, 50, 51, 53, 54, 56, 59, 60, 61, 64, 65, 71, 72, 73, 75, 88, 93, 94, 96

It is more than appropriate that we should have photographed a book featuring the landscapes of Dorset. Dorset will always be our own county by virtue of birth but photographically it represents much more than that to both of us.

We have each photographed Dorset for more than twenty five years, predominantly to secure images for our audio visual programmes which we have performed widely throughout the county since 1968. Indeed the publication of this book has prompted the unveiling of a new programme exploring the landscapes of Dorset.

One sequence in particular, 'Hardy's Dorset', provided us with an opportunity to explore the heart of the county, much of it previously unknown to us.

In producing 'Hardy's Dorset' we were most fortunate in being guided through the county by a local author, the late Monica Hutchings, whose commentaries have accompanied our presentations and still provide an open window into Hardy's Dorset, more than twenty years after they were first recorded.

Monica once described Dorset as "a small, modest but most beautiful county which is not nearly so well known or appreciated as it deserves to be".

While photographing this book we have explored even further into our home county, discovering many new locations and images. The experience has been tremendously satisfying both photographically and spiritually. In terms of the actual ground covered we now feel we know every hill, lane and tree in the county! Doubtless, however, Dorset will continue to hold many more surprises for us in future assignments.

Our fervent hope is that this book will provide its readers with a thought provoking appreciation of this county's countryside. As photographers, it affords us the opportunity of saying 'Thank you Dorset' for providing us with images of a county which despite the ravages of man, will retain its position in most people's minds as the epitome of rural beauty.

Roger Holman and Roger Lane
SEPTEMBER 1991

PILSDON PEN AND FORDE ABBEY

West Dorset is a land of hills and vales, of trees and hedgerows, of green and narrow lanes and lonely, scattered farmsteads. In the face of twentieth century advancement, its landscape has changed less than most, perhaps less than any in the county. Its hollows and heights are much as they were when they impressed even the Lake District Wordworths, who came here in 1795.

"We have hills," wrote Dorothy, sister of William Wordsworth the poet, "which, seen from a distance, almost take on the character of mountains, some cultivated nearly to their summits, others in their wild state, covered with furze and broom. These delight me the most as they remind me of our native wilds." Their two years in Dorset were among the most productive of William's literary life. They lived at Racedown, a mile or two from Pilsdon Pen, the highest point in Dorset at 908 feet, with views, on a clear day, of the Mendips and Dartmoor and, closer to home, West Dorset's own Marshwood Vale.

Two thousand years before the Wordsworths, Pilsdon had other visitors, Iron Age Celts who settled there and built a hillfort. They were of the Durotriges tribe, who occupied the whole of Dorset and fiercely resisted the Roman arrival in AD 43. The conquest took years to complete and Pilsdon was probably one of the last Durotrigian forts to fall.

Pilsdon is a place of superlatives and so is Forde Abbey. Sir Frederick Treves called it an "exquisite monastic building" and "the object of greatest interest" on Dorset's west frontier; to Arthur Mee it was "as fine a house as any that stands on an English river". In a nation dotted with ruined abbeys, its very survival is special, with walls which have stood since the twelfth, thirteenth,

sixteenth and seventeenth centuries. It owes its existence to Adelicia de Brioncis, niece of William the Conqueror, who befriended Cistercian monks returning sadly to base after a failed mission to found a Devonshire abbey in 1141. She offered them the manor of Thorncombe and they built their monastery on the Dorset bank of the Axe instead. The dormitory range and chapter house survive from the early days, the abbot's hall and cloister from the time of the last Abbot Thomas Chard. He was unable to save his abbey from dissolution in 1539; but happily the building survives as one of Dorset's finest historical assets.

Forde Abbey, approached through an avenue of limes

View from Pilsdon Pen

A DORSET BIBLIOGRAPHY

Works consulted in the preparation of The Landscapes of Dorset

Ashley, Harry: *Dorset, A Portrait in Colour* (Countryside, 1986); Dorset Yarns (Countryside, 1988)

Barrett, John C., Richard Bradley and Martin Green: *Landscape, Monuments and Society, The Prehistory of Cranborne Chase* (Cambridge University, 1991)

Benfield, Eric: *Purbeck Shop, A Stoneworker's Story of Stone* (Ensign, 1990)

Blomfield, Richard: *Poole, Harbour, Heath and Islands* (Regency, 1984); Poole, Town and Harbour (Dorset Publishing, 1989)

Brett, Ernest J: *Six Men on the Stour* (Guttridge and Topp, 1985)

Brown, Mary: *Dorset Customs, Curiosities and Country Lore* (Ensign, 1990)

Cecil, David: *Some Dorset Country Houses* (Dovecote, 1985)

Chandler, John: *Wessex Images* (Sutton, 1990)

Clark, Geoffrey and W. Harding Thompson: *The Dorset Landscape* (Black, 1935)

Darton, F. J. Harvey: *The Marches of Wessex* (Newnes, 1922, 1936)

Davies, G. M: *The Dorset Coast, A Geological Guide* (Black, 1935)

Davis, Terence: *Wareham, Gateway to Purbeck* (Dorset Publishing, 1984)

Draper, Jo: *Dorset, The Complete Guide* (Dovecote, 1986); Thomas Hardy, A Life in Pictures (Dovecote, 1989)

Gardiner, Dorothy: *Companion into Dorset* (Methuen, 1937)

Gibb, J. H. P: *The Book of Sherborne* (Barracuda, 1981)

Good, Ronald: *The Lost Villages of Dorset* (Dovecote, 1979, 1987)

Guttridge, Roger: *Dorset Smugglers* (Dorset Publishing, 1984); Dorset Murders (Gasson 1986, Ensign 1990); *Ten Dorset Mysteries* (Ensign, 1989); *Blackmore Vale Camera* (Dovecote, 1991)

Hardy, Thomas: *The Return of the Native* (1878); *Tess of the d'Urbervilles* (1891)

Hawkins, Desmond: *Cranborne Chase* (Gollancz, 1981)

Hills, Catherine: *Blood of the British, From Ice Age to Norman Conquest* (George Philip, 1986)

Hutchings, Monica: *Dorset River* (Macdonald, 1956)

Jenkins, Elizabeth: *Jane Austen* (Gollancz, 1987)

Legg, Rodney: *Purbeck Island* (Dorset Publishing, 1972, 1989); *Exploring the Heartland of Purbeck* (Dorset Publishing, 1986); *Brownsea, Dorset's Fantasy Island* (Dorset Publishing, 1986); *Dorset at War, Diary of WW2* (Dorset Publishing, 1986, 1990); *Lulworth and Tyneham Revisited* (Dorset Publishing, 1985); *National Trust Dorset* (Dorset Publishing, 1987); *Purbeck's Heath* (Dorset Publishing, 1987); *Literary Dorset* (Dorset Publishing, 1990);

Leighton, Brian: *A Short History of Tyneham*

Mee, Arthur (ed): *Dorset* (Hodder & Stoughton, 1939); *Hampshire with the Isle of Wight* (Hodder & Stoughton, 1939)

Mills, A. D: *Dorset Place-Names, Their Origins and Meanings* (Gasson 1986, Ensign 1990)

Morris, Stuart: *Portland: An Illustrated History* (Dovecote, 1985)

National Trust, The: *Corfe Castle* (National Trust, 1988)

New Dorset Bird Club: *Dorset Birds 1989* (New Dorset Bird Club, 1990)

Newman, John and Nikolaus Pevsner: *The Buildings of England: Dorset* (Penguin, 1972)

Newman, Sue: *Lives and Times of a Victorian House in Christchurch* (Newman, 1991)

Osborne, George: *Dorset Curiosities* (Dovecote, 1986)

Peters, John (ed: Roger Guttridge): *Bournemouth Then and Now, A Pictorial Past* (revised edition Ensign, 1990)

Pitfield, F. P: *Dorset Parish Churches A-D* (Dorset Publishing, 1981)

Pridham, Llewellyn Pridham and Edwin Kestin: *The Dorset Coastline* (Longmans)

Putnam, Bill: *Roman Dorset* (Dovecote, 1984)

Roscoe, Ernest (ed): *The Marn'll Book* (Blackmore, 1952)

Sale, Richard and Tom Ang: *Dorset* (Hutchinson, 1985)

Savage, Anne (translator/collator): *The Anglo-Saxon Chronicles* (Heinemann, 1982)

Short, Bernard C: *A Short History of Brownsea Island* (Looker, 1965)

Treves, Sir Frederick: *Highways and Byways in Dorset* (Macmillan, 1906, 1935)

Vesey-Fitzgerald, Brian: *Hampshire and the Isle of Wight* (Hale, 1949)

Wallis, A. J: *Dorset Bridges, A History and Guide* (Abbey Press, 1974)

Wansbrough, Richeldis: *The Tale of Milton Abbas* (Dorset Publishing, 1974)

PHOTOGRAPHING THE LANDSCAPES OF DORSET

Most dictionaries define 'landscape' as 'an art reproduction of an actual place' but in photographic terms can it mean rather more than that? What, for example, makes one landscape photograph stand out more than another?

Some landscapes are little more than a pictorial record but the classic landscape has to be that one image you can keep looking at time and time again, that one image which even the photographer knows would be difficult to repeat. Such an image is scarce indeed.

Landscapes can also be quite emotive. Some will elate the viewer while others can depress. Quite why this should be is difficult to analyse. For some people mountains can appear dramatic and uplifting but others see them as domineering and oppressive. Whether painter or photographer your reaction to the scene and the emotion you felt at the time will invariably appear in your painting or photograph and will almost certainly be transmitted to the viewer.

Perhaps the power of the image and the way in which a photograph can produce an emotion is a measure of its success.

Just consider for a while the millions of holiday pictures taken every year and ask why were they all taken. If they were merely to provide a record of a place visited, would not a postcard have proved a worthwhile purchase? Not at all, because those holiday photographs are saying something more than 'this is where we've been', they are saying something of the way the photographer felt when the shutter was pressed. Doubtless those same feelings will return when the holiday photographs are viewed sometime in the future.

So it is with landscape photography. The way landscapes appeal to each individual can be captured by the camera and communicated or shared with others.

Photographic images can be extremely powerful but for the photographer the creation of those very special images remains a quest for that elusive moment when light and land combine to produce a scene of unique quality. Witnessing such a moment can be an emotive experience as indeed can any gift of nature but to capture that moment on film is to discover photography in its truest form.

So just how do we set about capturing that classic landscape photograph? Without doubt it is a long hard road of dedication, frustration, elation and disappointment. Just occasionally there is an element of surprise and even luck.

We won't concern ourselves with equipment and technicalities at this stage, after all perception is the key, our eyes are the most important piece of equipment we can possess. Recognising that special moment when sunlight and cloud paint patterns on the landscape is the first step to creating a successful picture.

To experience the effect of light on the landscape, visit a favourite location and just quietly observe the scene. It really is a case of watching and waiting, it is impossible to tell precisely what is going to happen. Sometimes the wind will break up clouds at different levels allowing sunshine through to create shapes of light on the land. There may be just one fleeting moment when the light possesses a very special character which photography has

(continued on page 20)

Fire was Beaminster's greatest enemy in the past, for the town suffered three major conflagrations between 1644 and 1781. But yesterday's foe can be today's friend and reconstruction has created a town of rare neatness and beauty, built in local limestone and earning the admiration of allcomers. The bow windows of the late Georgian Pines Gallery in Fleet Street are a gem among gems.

When Sir Frederick Treves came to Beaminster in Edwardian times, many of the buildings were still comparatively new, yet even his normally caustic pen could find only praise for the town in the "great hollow" beneath the road from Toller Whelme.

Fleet Street, Beaminster, showing the finest of many fine frontages

"Beaminster," he wrote, "is a clean, cheerful, self-respecting county town, without pretensions, without offensively modern houses, and without red-brick suburbs. There are a few thatched cottages in the streets, but Beaminster mostly affects a cosy, yellow-brown stone and ruddy tiles for its dwelling places." Happily, little has changed in ninety years.

From a slope of the hollow, one of Dorset's tallest church towers rises 100 feet from the ground, boasting a rich assortment of pinnacles, gargoyles and other carvings which was even richer before the ravages of Reformation or perhaps the Civil War. St Mary's tower has a second claim to fame, a macabre one, for in 1685 the quartered remains of men were suspended there, members of Monmouth's makeshift army executed and exhibited for their part in a rebellion by the late king's illegitimate son. West Dorset supplied a large proportion of Monmouth's rebels and many paid with their lives at the bloody hands of Lord Chief Justice Jeffreys.

Beaminster has a history of hauntings, too, and the best-documented case again concerns St Mary's Church. Here in 1728 a group of boys saw the ghost of their recently departed friend John Daniel in the gallery which served as their schoolroom. The thirteen-year-old was "sitting at his writing desk where he used to sit when living". Daniel's death was suspicious, the apparition prompted exhumation and an inquest jury decided he had been murdered. The prime suspect was his step-mother but there was insufficient evidence to justify a trial.

Beaminster... the town in the hollow

the power to capture in an instant. If however, the light remains unchanging and dull, resist the temptation to leave and go in search of another location. Nature can and often will play the strangest tricks with light, and usually when your back is turned. Rather like a fisherman, you just have to sit there waiting for a catch.

Unexplored territory can stimulate and sharpen up the visual senses but there really is no substitute for an in-depth knowledge of an area. Knowing where some muddy track may lead and what view can be experienced at the end of it can be a major asset when trying to get that different view or aspect of a familiar scene.

Repeat visits to the same location are also important, particularly at different times of the day or season of the year. The position of and height of the sun throughout the year will provide many different images from the same viewpoint.

Winter light can be particularly conducive to landscape photography, yet winter is traditionally the time of year when most camera shutters stay silent.

During the winter months when the sun is lower, the shadows of the trees and the contours of the hills are far more pronounced, adding more texture and relief to the scene. Photograph that same scene again at the same time but on a summer's day and notice the difference. It will almost certainly be lacking in shadow, relief and texture, merely a record of the location and definitely not an "art reproduction of an actual place".

It is this very reason which makes landscape photography

more successful early in the morning and late in the afternoon. During the middle of the day the sun is at its highest and produces no modelling of the landscape.

Is it really all to do with light? Just what makes the difference between an evocative landscape photograph and one which is merely a pictorial record?

For the most part it is the quality of the light, after all photography has often been called "painting with light". Next must be composition which is entirely in the hands of the photographer. The eye must search every corner of the viewfinder, eliminating those elements which do not contribute to the overall composition.

It is most unlikely that a magnificent view photographed with a wide angle lens will make a striking photograph, the photographer must be selective. By closely observing the scene and choosing an aspect or detail which may say something about the region, country or place will prove a major contribution to a successful picture.

The sky also plays an important part, in fact there may be occasions when the colour of the sky and the shape of the clouds is so attractive it becomes the main reason for taking the photograph. Alternatively, the patterns and shapes of pebbles on a sea shore may have caught your eye; here the horizon can be placed high in the picture focusing attention on the foreground.

Foreground interest in particular will always enhance and provide depth to a picture, it will lead the eye into the main aspect.

(continued from page 20)

Landscape photography is not just distant vistas: woodland scenes, a canopy of leaves, the bark of a tree and reflections in a river are all subjects which can produce a memorable photograph.

Weather of course does play an essential role but when the wind is howling and the rain crashing on the window at five o'clock in the morning, the dedicated photographer doesn't go back to sleep, he ventures out as planned. Weather is a fickle element, particularly in Britain and is likely to change before a chosen location is reached.

The quest for that elusive landscape cannot always be achieved by driving around in a car; a photographer must be prepared to walk for long periods continually captivated by what image lies over that hill or around the next cove.

Photographing the landscape can be an enormously pleasurable experience. When that final image has the power to communicate the photographer's emotions to the viewer it will have been successful, but if the photographer can keep looking at that image time and time again, a landscape will have been created and perhaps even an art reproduction of an actual place.

BATCOMBE HILL AND UPCERNE

Of all Dorset's geological features, chalk has the greatest single influence on the landscape, for its great rolling hills dominate a third of the county. It enters Dorset from Wiltshire and Hampshire in the north-east, forms a broad diagonal belt of downland across the middle and mid-west of the county and sticks out a south-easterly limb to meet the sea on either side of Lulworth and north of Swanage. Between the hills are rich clay vales, which were marshy, forested areas when men first moved in and began the process of clearance and drainage.

Batcombe Hill is on the edge of the chalk and overlooks much of north-west Dorset. On its lower slopes are Hillfield, which has an extant friary, and Batcombe, whose church, until the end of the last century, was missing one of the four pinnacles which originally graced its tower. Its loss, apparently, was the work of one Conjuror Minterne, a seventeenth century squire who owed his nickname to his legendary dealings with the devil. Once, according to the natives of these rural parts, he leapt from the crest of the hill on his noble steed and attempted to clear the church at the bottom. But his calculations must have been slightly adrift for the horse's trailing hoof clipped the top of the tower and the pinnacle was thus removed.

On Batcombe Hill is another object which has fired the imaginations of country folk, an oval stone pillar, nearly feet high and known as the Cross and Hand. Some say it was the scene of a murder, others the scene of a miracle, yet others that it provided alms for needy travellers. Hardy's Tess was told a fourth theory, concerning the torture and burial of a malefactor, but the stone's true purpose was probably to mark a boundary in Roman or Saxon times.

Upcerne is also a village of the central Dorset chalk, lying "among the downs smiling to itself like a child in hiding, delighted that the highroad passes so near yet misses it", as Arthur Mee and friends put it in 1939. Architecturally its finest asset is a gabled manor house built at the beginning of the seventeenth century.

Thatched cottage at Upcerne

Batcombe Hill above Hillfield

THE EQUIPMENT — A BRIEF REVIEW

There is no ideal camera for landscape photography; however there are numerous classic landscape images gracing the pages of books, magazines and even on walls which have been produced with the ubiquitous 35mm camera.

The universal appeal and capability of the modern 35mm camera is well known and in recent years the 'auto everything' compact camera has brought high quality image creation into the hands of a much wider population.

The more discerning photographer will always strive for maximum image quality. In landscape photography that means either a large format camera capable of producing an image size of 5" x 4" on sheet film or a medium format roll film camera with a choice of either 6 x 6 cm square image or a range from 6 x 4.5 to 6 x 9 cm. The majority of images in this book have been taken with medium format Bronica cameras, Roger Holman using the 6 x 6 cm square format and Roger Lane the 6 x 4.5 cm image size. The choice is somewhat subjective and largely depends on whether the photographer feels comfortable composing an image within a square frame.

Medium format cameras and lenses are essentially larger, bulkier and heavier than 35mm equipment and for this reason alone it is essential to keep lenses and accessories to a minimum.

After all there is much walking involved in search of that classic landscape image, perhaps much of it uphill or over unstable terrain.

Most landscape photographers develop a 'seeing eye' with one particular favourite lens. In this respect Roger Holman uses a 40mm wide angle lens to creat a foreground interest and lead in the eye while Roger Lane enjoys a 150mm medium telephoto lens to select an element of the landscape which has appealed to him. Good landscape photography can be achieved with the use of just one lens, usually the standard lens which in medium format terms is a 75mm or 80mm focal length. The use of additional lenses will however, allow the photographer to extend or vary the viewpoint, perspective and composition.

The use of filters in landscape photography can be a rather emotive and controversial subject. On this subject both Rogers agree and use filters with a great deal of restraint, preferring at all times to record an image as naturally as possible. Just occasionally they will improve a weak featureless sky with the delicate hue of a graduated filter, usually a "grey" or "sunset pink". The most common filter they each use is a Polariser. When placed in front of the lens and rotated to a certain position, it will block out ultra violet light. Since the sky contains a large amount of ultra violet, it will become a darker blue in the final image, grass will also appear slightly greener and all colours will generally appear more saturated. The only other filters they employ are Skylight filters which stay on their lenses at all times. These filters produce a minimal warming effect on colours but also play a valuable role in protecting the lens from nature's elements, particularly dust and sea spray.

Both Rogers agree that without question the most useful piece of equipment they employ in landscape photography is a tripod.

Certainly tripod weight and handling does require a certain discipline to persevere with its use. The advantages however are soon recognised and use of a tripod becomes second nature.

But perhaps the most useful aspect of a tripod is the one which is least evident. A tripod actually slows the photographer down and that discipline of taking just a little more time, focuses attention toward the stronger elements of composition. Working more slowly will also allow the photographer to feel more relaxed, allowing both landscape and photography to be enjoyed even more, and that must be revealed in the pictures.

In an age of tanker terminals and container ports, it is hard to imagine little Lyme Regis as a port of consequence, yet three centuries ago it was the fourteenth largest in England. It has no natural harbour, making do with a man-made alternative, the Cobb, whose history is almost as old as the town itself. As long ago as 1250, the present Cobb's medieval ancestor was sheltering the town's fishing fleet from the winds and waves of the open Channel. It was mainly a wooden structure then, comprising lines of huge oak piles sunk into the seabed, forming the bread of a sandwich with great loose stones as its filling. The Cobb has been lost to storms several times over the centuries, the last occasion

Lyme Regis... "a pretty market town set in the roots of a high rocky hill down to the hard shore"

in 1825, when it was rebuilt in its present form in Portland stone.

Like its Cobb, Lyme's borough status dates from the reign of Edward I, from whom it obtained the right to call itself "Regis" – "Lyme of the King". Appropriately for a royal haven, it went on to witness some of history's great events and to feature in two great works of literature. From the hills above the town in 1588, the locals watched the opening skirmishes with the Spanish Armada, proud that Lyme itself had provided two vessels for Elizabeth's fighting fleet. In the Civil War the town survived an eight-week siege before being relieved by its Parliamentary allies. In 1685 came the dramatic daybreak landing of the Duke of Monmouth, come to claim the throne of England. His seven boatloads of armed men were at first mistaken for an invading force but the claimant's rhetoric moved the yokels and he left Lyme with an army of thousands. Many lived long enough to rue the day, but little longer.

In modern times Lyme has carved a career in tourism and small yachts and pleasure craft now rub fenders with the working boats which still regard the Cobb as home. Two novelists have assisted the cause – Jane Austen, who stayed here and described the town in Persuasion, and John Fowles, who lives here and featured Lyme in The French Lieutenant's Woman. Part of Lyme's charm is its quaintness of character, fundamentally unaltered since John Leland's mid-sixteenth century visit. "Lyme is a pretty market town set in the roots of a high rocky hill down to the hard shore," he wrote. "There cometh a shallow brook from the hills about three miles by north, and cometh fleeting on great stones through a stone bridge in the bottom."

Lyme from its artificial harbour known as the Cobb

THE AUTHOR

ROGER GUTTRIDGE, born in 1950, was brought up in the Sturminster Newton area of North Dorset, educated at Blandford Grammar School and now lives at Wimborne. He has been a journalist in the area since 1970, first with The Western Gazette and later the Bournemouth Evening Echo, of which he is a former chief reporter. He is now a freelance writer based at Wimborne. His other books include Dorset Smugglers, Dorset Murders, Ten Dorset Mysteries, Hampshire Murders, Blackmore Vale Camera and, as editor, Bournemouth Then and Now (by John Peters) and Six Men on the Stour (by Ernest J. Brett). He also writes the popular Heritage columns in the Bournemouth and Southern Evening Echoes. Roger Guttridge is married to Sylvie and has one son, Andrew.

Roger Lane (left)
Roger Guttridge and
Roger Holman (right).

THE PHOTOGRAPHERS

ROGER HOLMAN was born near Wimborne in 1932 and brought up in the area before entering the family electrical business, Holman Radio and Television, of which he is now managing director. Photography has been his lifelong hobby, an interest which began when he was still a teenager and had progressed by the 1960s to audio-visual productions on such topics as Hardy's Dorset, the Isle of Purbeck and the Changing Face of Wimborne. In this work he found an equally talented collaborate in Roger Lane and their audio-visuals are now well-known and widely admired in Dorset, where they continue to attract large audiences at every showing. In 1990 Roger Holman decided for the first time to enter one of his photographs for an award. The chosen picture featured Fiddleford Mill and was submitted for the Best of Britain 1990 competition, sponsored by the magazine People in Camera and judged by film producer David Puttnam and royal photographer Lord Lichfield. From an entry of 5,261 photographs, Roger Holman's was adjudged the best in the Beautiful Britain category in the amateur section, the best in all five categories for amateur photographers and the best in all categories – professional, amateur and student – to win the Best of Britain 1990 award. The award-winning picture appears opposite the title page in The Landscapes of Dorset. Roger Holman is married to Rosemary, has three sons, Gary, Paul and Steven, and a daughter, Julie, and lives near Wimborne.

ROGER LANE was born in Dorset in 1945, has lived in the Wimborne area all his life and works as administration manager for a local aerospace company. He became interested in photography in the mid-1960s and in 1967 joined Wimborne Camera Club, where Roger Holman was among his fellow members. The two Rogers, with Ian Bigg, became involved in photographic teach-ins at Avon Tyrrell in the New Forest, which became a major event in the UK photographic calendar and attracted many leading photographers. Audio-visual productions followed, later under the name Coloursound, and the group was the first to introduce foreign audio-visuals to the UK. Roger Lane's first audio-visual was Race, commissioned in 1968 by Agfa-Gevaert. He then worked on other audio-visuals – including Hardy's Dorset and The Isle of Purbeck – with Roger Holman and the well-known Dorset writer Monica Hutchings. Later productions included Steamdream, based on the paintings and railways of wildlife artist David Shepherd, with commentary by the late Wynford Vaughan-Thomas, and most recently In Pursuit of Nature, a portrait of Claude Monet and the landscapes in which he worked. Roger Lane's work has now progressed to freelance writing and photography for magazines. He is married to Maria, has one son, Mark, and lives near Wimborne.

CHARMOUTH AND EGGARDON HILL

Jane Austen knew Charmouth, and loved it, describing its "sweet, retired bay, backed by dark cliffs, where fragments of low rock among the sands make it the happiest spot for watching the flow of the tide, for sitting in unwearied contemplation". Mary Anning also knew Charmouth but was concerned less with its atmosphere and natural beauty than with the offerings of the fossil-rich lias cliffs. In 1811, a few years after Jane Austen's visit, eleven-year-old Miss Anning became the first person to set eyes on an ichthyosaur's skeleton, establishing her fame as the Fossil Woman of Lyme and the area's fame as a fossil hunter's paradise.

Those same dark cliffs that Jane Austen described have seen their share of history, especially in ancient times, when the peace of Charmouth's shore and valley was disturbed more than once. The Danes landed here in 833, driving back King Egbert of Wessex and his Saxon forces. They came again in 840, forcing King Ethelwulf to retreat. Both battles were bloody and even the victors had no stomach for more, preferring to sail away in their longboats to nurse their wounds unhindered.

More blood was spilled a thousand years later but the combatants in 1825 were coastguards and smugglers. The coastguards were attacked "with great violence"; they fired on the smugglers and one of them fell and was dragged away; then his comrades retaliated by throwing rocks from the clifftop. Such incidents were not uncommon for this was prime smuggling country and smuggling was big business in the eighteenth and early nineteenth centuries.

Eggardon Hill, some miles to the north-east, also has a smuggling connection, for it's said that the smuggler Isaac Gulliver planted a pine clump here as a navigation point for his ships approaching the Dorset coast. The trees were eventually felled on Government orders but traces remain of the octagonal earthwork built to protect the saplings from the winds which sweep across the hill 820 feet above sea level.

Like Charmouth, Eggardon has an ancient history, for its great green ramparts once supported the defensive wooden walls of an Iron Age village. The hillfort dates from about 300 BC and was taken over by invading Romans three-and-a-half centuries later. It stands on the front line of Dorset's chalk uplands, offering spectacular views of the Marshwood Vale and beyond.

The ancient camp of Eggardon Hill

Sunrise at Charmouth

THE HEADLAND OF GOLDEN CAP

Standing bold and proud between Charmouth and Bridport is the headland of Golden Cap, at 618 feet the highest sea cliff in southern England. Its scale alone is impressive but its natural beauty ensures a greater fame. On a sunny day its golden crest of upper greensand, protected by a lid of chert, glints and glistens in the sunlight, contrasting with the darker blues and greys of the Eype clay cliffs below.

Golden Cap today enjoys National Trust protection for it was bought in 1978 in memory of Lord Antrim, the trust's chairman for eleven years. The trust owns 2,000 acres in these parts, including five or six coastal miles and, inland, Dorset's highest hill, the 908-foot hillfort Pilsdon Pen beyond the Marshwood Vale. Human threats to the best of West Dorset's landscapes have thus receded but the elements pose a greater threat for the coast is prone to landslips like those at Cain's Folly and the cliff falls which provide a continual supply of fossils from the fragile blue lias cliffs between Golden Cap and Lyme.

Beyond West Bay, layered cliffs of soft Bridport sand rise sheer from a beach of fine shingle (see page 10). East Cliff is followed by Burton Cliff, whose shore marks the true commencement of the Chesil Beach, though not of course the Fleet. Strangely, there is no bay at West Bay but there is a harbour of sorts which has served generations of Bridport fishing folk and netmakers. Sir Frederick Treves thought it "probably the queerest seaport in any part of the British Isles" with a harbour barely big enough to accommodate a schooner, a ketch and sundry rowing boats, yet equipped with "mighty rings and bollards to hold the leviathians of the deep".

"The waterway to the port is a mere gully hacked through the beach and marked by two wooden piers of the ruggedest type," wrote Treves. "Any ship the size of a schooner has to be dragged into the harbour by ropes and has to be coaxed between the piers." Since Treves' time West Bay has made its way in the world as a seaside resort, albeit one of modest dimensions. Its buildings cluster around the eighteenth century harbour in a way more reminiscent of Cornwall or Kent than of Dorset.

Golden Cap from Lyme Regis

CHESIL BEACH AND ST. CATHERINE'S CHAPEL

The Chesil Beach is not so much a piece of coastline, more a natural wonder of the world. For a million years it has greedily reaped a harvest from the tidal ebb and flow, always adding to its store of pebbles, giving few away. They come in many forms, from the rocks of many places, some of them far distant. If it were possible to weigh them, they would tip the scales at fifty million tons; if it were possible to load them into lorries, the convoy would stretch from England to Australia. Moving west from Portland, the pebbles become progressively smaller, sifted and graded by the waves to reach a state of fine shingle beneath the cliffs of Burton Bradstock and Bridport, which some say mark the true western end of Chesil Beach. Smugglers and fishermen stepping ashore in fog or darkness had only to take a handful of pebbles to know where they had landed.

Scientists, over the years, have propounded a catalogue of theories as to how the beach was formed but locals have their own explanation, as handed down from father to son and mother to daughter. They believe the beach was raised in a single night by a most ferocious storm, though neither they nor their ancestors were here to see it. Working in harness, storms, tides and the Chesil Beach are a deadly team and no-one knows how many lives have been sacrificed on this eighteen-mile altar of pebbles. Deadman's Bay is Thomas Hardy's name for the sea enclosed by the curving coastline, a kind of black hole of the Channel from which, in certain conditions in the days of sail, no ship returned. Occasionally the pebble barrier itself is breached, as in 1824, when most of Fleet village and its medieval church were swept away in an incident adopted by J. Meade Falkner for his novel Moonfleet.

Yet Chesil Beach and the Fleet, its eight-mile part-freshwater part-brackish lagoon, have also offered rich pickings for many, and not only for the wreckers who swooped hyena-like whenever an ill-starred vessel struck the shore. Mackerel fishing with seine nets is a traditional industry here and three centuries ago Daniel Defoe wrote of catches so large that the fish sold "for a hundred a penny". The Fleet is to ornithologists what the cliffs of Lyme and Charmouth are to fossil-hunters; the beach provides a similar service for beachcombers as the remains of long-sunken ships release their long-forgotten treasures from the bed of Deadman's Bay.

St Catherine's Chapel, Chesil Beach, the Fleet and Portland

View from the Chesil Beach as storm clouds gather over Portland

THE LIGHTHOUSE AT PORTLAND

Dorset is a county of greens and yellows, purples and blues, but at Portland Bill the lighthouse stands, conspicuous and purposeful, in a flared gown of red and white. There has been a lighthouse here since 1716, when twin towers were erected at different levels to offer ships a clear bearing by night and day. The coal-fired towers were run by private enterprise and made huge profits by levying dues on passing vessels, payable at the next port of call, with surplus profits going to charity.

It took years of lobbying to obtain permission for the first twin lighthouses, though Portland's coastal waters, its rocks and sandbank, its Race and treacherous currents, had been a mariners' graveyard since ancient times. In 1789 Portland's twin towers played an important role in the development of lighthouses everywhere. The higher tower became the first lighthouse in Britain to have Argand lamps with their oil-fired wicks housed in a glass tube and their flames intensified by polished reflectors; the lower tower was rebuilt in a different form on a different site to become, after a series of experiments, the world's first lighthouse to project its light through a true lens. "The light from the six Argand lamps was concentrated into a series of intensely brilliant fixed beams, each easily reaching eighteen miles to the seaward horizon on a clear night," says Portland historian Stuart Morris.

The present lighthouse, built in 1905, towers 135 feet above a landscape of sea and stone, huts and cafes and a vast, bare car park. Its huge revolving light is impressive and the

energetic can climb 153 steps to see it. At ground level is an inscription preserved for 200 years: "For the direction and comfort of navigators, for the benefit and security of commerce. A lasting memorial of British hospitality to all nations. This lighthouse was erected by the ancient corporation of Trinity House of Deptford Strond in 1798."

Portland Bill snack bar in matching decor

The lighthouse at
Portland Bill

Portland is another of Dorset's geographical oddities. It stands almost 500 feet above the sea, rugged, bleak and treeless and protected by steep cliffs. Hardy called it "a huge lump of freestone", the "Gibraltar of Wessex"; Victor Hugo saw it as a bird's head laid on its side in the sea. It is called an island but is not one, for the connecting thread of Chesil Beach denies it true island status. Yet its natives have the minds of islanders, and the customs, too.

Since ancient times Portlanders have made good use of their most plentiful resource, the vast lump of oolite rock beneath their feet. "The people be good there in flinging of stones, and use it for defence of the isle," John Leland noted in 1540. Parts of Portland today are scarred by centuries of quarrying, an ancient industry revived and greatly expanded after it was chosen by Inigo Jones for the rebuilding of the Whitehall Banqueting Hall in 1619.

For centuries Portland was also famous for its hardy black-faced sheep, which roamed freely across the sloping, windswept plateau and produced the best mutton in England. "The natives were as hardy and as well defined a race as the sheep," wrote Treves in 1906. "They had little traffic with the mainland, where they were regarded as recluses of unpleasant habits. The Portlanders not only kept to themselves, but were exceedingly jealous of strangers; they married only with their own folk, and possessed curious laws and still more curious morals."

One of the curious customs Treves was referring to was sex before marriage which, far from being forbidden, even in Victorian times, was actively encouraged. If the girl became pregnant, she told her mother, who told her father, who told her lover and arranged a wedding. If pregnancy failed to occur within a reasonable time, the courtship was abandoned and the parties sought more productive liaisons elsewhere.

With the customs go quaint superstitions, one of them shared with mariners from the French province of Brittany, who also believe that mention of a certain member of the animal kingdom invites bad luck. "Monks introduced a little furry creature with long ears from France in the twelfth century," Portland historian Stuart Morris notes diplomatically. We may add, without jeopardising sales on the "isle", that the creature's name begins with an "r" and ends with a "t" and is not rat.

Portland Bill

Portland from Came Down

THE CHURCH OF ST GEORGE, REFORNE

A curiosity among Dorset churches is the grand St George's, standing splendidly alone at Reforne, near Easton, on Portland's windswept top. Newman and Pevsner call it the most impressive eighteenth century church in the county, Draper considers it "superb but eccentric", Treves quotes another who said it was "built in an indescribable quasi-classical style of eighteenth century architecture, midway between Wren and a Byzantine basilica".

St George's unique design was the brainchild of a Portland gentleman, Thomas Gilbert, grandson of Sir Christopher Wren's quarry agent of seventy years before. It was begun in 1754 to replace the collapsed St Andrew's, completed in 1766, abandoned in 1917, restored to its former glory in the 1970s. "It is a large, self-consciously monumental building of ashlar with a Wrenian west tower, a stunted dome, an apse, and transepts," adds Pevsner.

In the churchyard at Reforne inscribed limestone gravestones, neglected and dripping with ivy, reflect the harsher sides of life on the rugged rock and the savagery of the sea which pounds Portland's deadly cliffs. Here in 1803 was brought the body of Mary Way, aged eighteen, one of several Portlanders "shot by some of a press gang", as her headstone puts it. The gang came in search of manpower for the Navy but met resistance in Easton Square. Shots were exchanged, nine marines injured, two quarrymen and a blacksmith shot dead, two other natives, including Mary Way, badly wounded. Mary lingered seven weeks before dying of her wounds.

An even greater tragedy occurred in heavy seas in 1877

St George's churchyard

when two ships collided in Deadman's Bay. The Avalanche, bound for New Zealand, sank in seconds, many of its sixty-three passengers and thirty-four crew trapped in their berths, others scrambling desperately to make the deck. The Forest, manned by a crew of twenty-one and bound for New York, was was also holed, and lodged bow-down on a sandbank. Next morning, when the disaster was discovered, Portland fishermen mounted a heroic rescue operation, risking their own lives in the still heaving seas. Only twelve people had survived, nine crewmen from the Forest, three from the Avalanche. Of the 106 who perished, many of them whole families, only six were washed ashore, and these buried in the churchyard of St George.

St George's Church, Reforne, Portland

It is neither the biggest town in Dorset nor the most handsome, yet Dorchester – the Casterbridge of Hardy – is a place well worthy of its status as the county town. Its pedigree is impressive, both in history and in literature, embracing great names, great events and a great span of years. It is a place bred to administer, a centre of civic importance from ancient times to our own. It has not one but two hillforts, Poundbury and the more impressive Maiden Castle, a place of Neolithic origin, where brave defenders of Iron Age Dorset were defeated by a superior army from Rome.

The Romans destroyed one great community here and created another, Durnovaria. It was their only town in Dorset, built on the slopes beside the river, where Dorchester stands today. Many reminders of Rome survive, including the remains of a town house in Colliton Park, mosaics in the county museum, walks following the lines of the old Roman walls, the Neolithic henge converted to a Roman amphitheatre and known today as Maumbury Rings.

Saxons, Normans and medieval English all took an interest in Dorchester, as did the Civil War Roundheads, who tapped a tidal wave of anti-Royalism on the western bank of the Frome. In the same century came two disasters, the first a destructive fire in 1613, the second a savage in judge's clothing, George Jeffreys, who sent twenty-nine to the gallows before lunch on the first morning of his Bloody Assize.

A more welcome visitor was Daniel Defoe, who in the 1720s found "a pleasant agreeable town to live in, and where I thought the people seem'd less divided into factions and parties than in other places".

The nineteenth century returned Dorchester to the frontline of both law and literature, the former through the Tolpuddle Martyrs, the latter through Hardy and Barnes. The martyrs were tried here in 1834 and sentenced to transportation for the crime of demanding a living wage. Trade unionists still honour their memory in the village of Tolpuddle each July.

Thomas Hardy, architect, novelist and poet, and William Barnes, parson, schoolmaster and author of dialect poems, both lived and wrote in Dorchester, and still live there in statue form. Kennington's Hardy sits in High West Street, his hat on his knees, an old man at peace with the world; Parson Barnes stands by St Peter's Church, a composed and dignified reincarnation in bronze by Roscoe Mullins.

The statue of William Barnes the poet, Dorchester

The River Frome and Dorchester viewed from the east

MILTON ABBEY: CHURCH, SCHOOL AND ALMSHOUSE

Where today the smooth green lawns of Milton Abbey stretch themselves extravagantly between wooded slopes, there once stood the houses and taverns of a medieval town. In so open and peaceful a setting it is hard to imagine the hustle and bustle which went on here centuries ago. The town's proper name was Middleton and it boasted one of the best and biggest markets in Dorset, attracting buyers and sellers from miles around. There was a market cross surrounded by thirty-two steps of stone, a successful brewery and a tapestry of streets woven around an abbey founded as long ago as AD 937.

It was a thriving community, yet one with a traumatic destiny. The original abbey was destroyed by fire in a thunder-storm in 1309 and rebuilt over many years. Then came the dissolution of monasteries, when the monks departed and lawyer Sir John Tregonwell moved in, rewarded for his help in the disposal of the king's wives. One of his descendants achieved fame at the age of five by falling from the church tower and parachuting to earth with the aid of his stiff petticoats; another founded the holiday town of Bournemouth.

Fate kept Middleton's greatest trauma for the eighteenth century, when a squire whose wealth was matched only by his arrogance decided that the town was "too close to his residence, and proved an annoyance". He solved the problem by removing it – the town, that is. Brick by brick, stone by stone, the houses were dismantled and demolished. The inns went the same way, along with the brewery, the Rectory, the almshouses and most of the medieval house which the Tregonwells had occupied. Even the gravestones in the churchyard were broken up and removed,

The Almshouses, Milton Abbas

as were the bones of dead Middletonians which inconsiderately turned up in the topsoil.

To house himself, Lord Milton, later Earl of Dorchester, built a new mansion on the site of the old one. It survives today as a public school, standing proud but almost alone on the vast lawn, its only structural companion being the fine Abbey Church built in the twelfth and fourteenth centuries. To house his dis-gruntled tenants, he built two rows of matching thatched cot-tages, out of sight, out of earshot and probably out of mind. Ironi-cally, the squire's high-handedness created a street which two centuries later is among the most picturesque in England.

The abbey church and and public school at Milton Abbas

CERNE ABBAS: GIANT AND GATEHOUSE

Cerne Abbas is like Milton Abbas might have been without Lord Milton's flagrant interference in its natural evolution. Like Milton alias Middleton, Cerne drew its early strength from its Abbey, founded by Aethelmar, Earl of Devon and Cornwall, in AD 987. "The holy house grew in power and magnificence, while about its walls sprang up a grateful town, only too eager to live upon the crumbs which fell from the rich monks' table," as Sir Frederick Treves put it. To Cerne Abbey in 1471 came Margaret of Anjou and her only son, seeking sanctuary after the capture of her husband King Henry VI and the defeat of his Lancastrian supporters. Weeks later mother and son were also taken prisoner at Tewkesbury and the boy murdered in cold blood.

Like Middleton, Cerne's Abbey stood in an amphitheatre of hills, gave birth to a flourishing market town, was reduced to ruin by the requirements of Henry VIII. Like Middleton, Cerne was overlooked in turn by the canal age, the railway age and the age of the juggernaut. But unlike Middleton, it was permitted to develop at its own pace so that its streets today are lined not by near-identical lifesize dolls' houses from the eighteenth century but by a varied and equally picturesque range of bowed, buckled and timbered frontages spanning five centuries of architectural styles. Cerne's church of St Mary is fifteenth century and there are remnants of the Abbey buildings at Abbey Farm.

Presiding over all from his hillside home is Cerne's oldest and largest resident, its famous chalk and turf giant. He stands 180 feet tall, brandishes a club of 120 feet and boasts manly assets which extend the tape measure to thirty feet. His age is unknown but he may be older than the Abbey itself; his name is uncertain and so is his raison d'etre. He could be the Greek god Hercules, as William Stukely claimed in 1764; or the pagan god Helith, as a Yorkshire monk asserted in 1297. Perhaps he represents a secret Celtic code or writing system, as Sydney Wood suggested in 1990; or perhaps he is simply the fertility symbol whose reputation lures childless couples up his chalk escarpment on moonless nights.

Cerne Abbas churchyard from the Abbey ruins

Cerne and its giant from Rowden Hill

THE FROME AT WOOL AND STINSFORD CHURCH

The Frome is second only to the Stour in the hierarchy of Dorset rivers; but unlike the Stour, it is also an exclusively Dorset product, beginning its journey in the hills near Evershot and ending it in the tidal shallows of Poole Harbour. Tess of the d'Urbervilles knew both rivers and her creator Thomas Hardy contrasted the "slow, silent, often turbid" streams of the Stour's Blackmore Vale with the clear and rapid waters of the Frome and its "pebbly shallows that prattled to the sky all day long".

Near Wool the Frome flows past the elegant and unspoilt Woolbridge Manor, built in the seventeenth century, and on through the five arches of Woolbridge itself, which dates from Tudor times. Both house and bridge were also known to Tess for it was here that she spent her disastrous honeymoon with Angel Clare. The old manor is a hotel now and faint traces of the hags' faces which frightened Hardy's tragic heroine can still be seen on the landing walls.

Woolbridge – which Hardy called Wellbridge – is a place associated more with his work than the man himself but at Stinsford, a few miles upstream, the reverse is true. Stinsford became Mellstock in his second published novel, Under the Greenwood Tree, but is best known as the village of his birth and upbringing. Hardy's home was at Higher Bockhampton, a hamlet within the parish, and it was to here that he returned at twenty-seven to write his early novels. He knew the church of Stinsford well, and loved it, despite his agnostic leanings. It held many memories for him, and strong family connections, and he wished to lie there beside his ancestors once the final chapter of his long life was written. But in death the power of Hardy's fame was greater than that of his last wish in life and he was denied the Stinsford burial he had sought. Instead, as a gruesome compromise, his heart was removed and buried there and his other remains cremated at Woking and buried in Poet's Corner at Westminster Abbey. Oddly, it is a poet of the next generation, the poet laureate Cecil Day Lewis, whose full remains lie at Stinsford, though his only link was a profession shared with the man whose heart, in life and in death, lay nearby.

The 13th century church at Stinsford

Woolbridge Manor and the River Frome

LULWORTH: THE CRUMPLE AND THE COVE

Four-and-a-half centuries ago the Tudor travel writer John Leland paused on his journey through England to admire the unique landscape of Lulworth, as countless travellers admire it today. He called it Lilleworth and described "on the shore a little fisher town where is a gut or creak out of the sea into the land, and is a succour for small ships". Some of the ships were probably pirate vessels for many in the sixteenth century regarded Lulworth as a principal port of call. Sheltered and remote, with natives whose co-operation could be easily bought, the Cove was well qualified for the role and carts loaded with piratical booty regularly rumbled northwards from here. The same qualities also served smugglers well and eighteenth century Lulworth was a notorious centre for contraband trade.

Rupert Brooke the poet came here early in the present century, and loved the place. Once, while reading in a boat off the rocks, he dropped his book overboard and jumped into the water to rescue it. The volume contained the work of another poet, John Keats, but it was not until four years later that Brooke discovered "the most amazing thing" – that Keats spent his last day in England at Lulworth in 1820, and wrote his last sonnet there.

Today's Lulworth Cove, no longer remote but possessed of a strange intimacy, is a target of tourists and trippers, attracted by the remarkable scenery and fine coastal walks. Here too is a geological battlefield, "a beautiful example of marine erosion in rocks of very unequal resistance", as G. M. Davies described it in his guide to Dorset's coastal geology. The more resistant rock is Portland Stone, which stands like the front line of a defending army, defying the enemy of wavepower, except at the Cove

Fishermen at Lulworth Cove

entrance, where the defensive lines were breached some time since, and the sea poured in and scooped out the sand and clay of the Wealden beds to create the Cove. Nearby is a cove in the making, Stair Hole. Here the battle is at its height, for the sea has carved arched entrances through the great stone wall and is eagerly devouring the soft terrain beyond. Soon, on a geological timescale, Stair Hole will become an extension of Lulworth Cove.

West of Stair Hole showing the "Lulworth crumple" in morning light

TWO VIEWS OF KIMMERIDGE

Kimmeridge is an industrial tease, a tempting resource whose cliffs and ledges of oily shale have flirted with entrepreneurs of every age, only to pull back if a relationship threatened to go too far. Stone Age men shaped the shale into ornaments, Romans turned it into jewellery and table legs. Smedmore's Elizabethan squire Sir William Clavell built a little pier and harbour here and began extracting alum from Kimmeridge Cliffs; he also made salt by boiling sea water and fuelled a glassworks by burning the shale; but all three enterprises ended in failure. Frenchmen of a later generation shipped the shale to Paris for use as gas, grease and lamp oil but the fumes proved offensive to Parisian nostrils and another scheme was stillborn. So were attempts to wring oil from the shale for the engines of the industrial nineteenth century.

Kimmeridge's failed flings with industry ensured the success of its marriage to nature and its waters today form part of a marine wildlife reserve. It also boasts a certain natural beauty, though the twentieth century's guidebook writers have proved strangely hard to please. Treves described the place as "desolate and dingy" with a "ridiculous tower" on the clifftop; Darton called it "grimy, slippery, unfriendly"; in our own time Jo Draper writes of the "rather depressing rock and limestone".

The tower which Treves so mockingly dismissed is Clavel's Tower, built by the Rev John Richards Clavell, who inherited Smedmore House and Estate in 1817. His folly stands on the clifftop to the east of Kimmeridge's modest beach, commanding fine views over Kimmeridge Bay. A little to the west are the old Coastguard cottages, built when a coastguard's main role in life was the prevention of smuggling. The Cooper family were among the more active smugglers here and tools of their trade – grappling irons and a brandy tub – can today be seen in the county museum at Dorchester.

Kimmeridge village is a mile inland and in the churchyard the remains of smugglers and coastguards lie side by side. Both professions were hazardous. Several gravestones stand in memory of coastguards who failed to reach the age of 25. Most were drowned while performing their duties or killed in accidents with firearms.

The oily cliffs of Kimmeridge in winter

Fishing at Kimmeridge

THE AGGLESTONE AND PURBECK HEATH

When Thomas Hardy described the "vast tract of unenclosed wild known as Egdon Heath", he was referring to the western block of heathland between Puddletown and Poole Harbour. Yet once this wild and primitive environment was even more vast, stretching almost unbroken across half the present county to link arms with the New Forest, its ally across the Hampshire border.

Hardy called the heathland untameable and named civilization as its enemy. The two have long been enemies, yet it was early civilization which gave birth to the heathland 4,000 years ago. Bronze Age farmers were responsible, for their clearance of the poor quality woodland upset the delicate balance of soil and plantlife, creating even poorer acid soil worthy only of gorse and heather.

Man gave Dorset its heathland wilderness and now it is man who takes it away. Farmers have nibbled at it since the seventeenth century, developers have devoured it since the nineteenth and gobbled it in the twentieth. Whole towns and sprawling suburbs have grown up on the heathland. Victorian Bournemouth itself was built where once was a carpet of heather; at Canford Heath and elsewhere the takeover continues, though today the heath has an increasingly powerful ally in public opinion.

Purbeck's heaths, though not unscathed, have suffered less than most, thanks partly to official protection. Studland Heath and Godlingston offer 1,500 acres of nature reserve to species in need of protection, including the smooth snake and sand lizard, Britain's two rarest reptiles. Here fire is the greatest enemy, though the heathland is not slow to regenerate.

The Purbeck Heath

Ancient men left more in these parts than acid soils for there are also barrows here and there and a stone circle of relatively modest dimensions at Rempstone. The Agglestone and its neighbour the Puckstone on Studland Heath have no known connection with prehistoric man but are lumps of ferruginous sandstone which have resisted the erosion which has afflicted the material around them. The Agglestone is the more impressive, measuring eighteen feet in height, eighty in circumference and weighing an estimated 500 tons. It has views of the sea and Poole Harbour and was a nesting site of ravens until the last century. Folklore tells us that the devil hurled it from the Isle of Wight – inaccurately, of course, for his target was Corfe Castle.

*Studland Heath and
the Agglestone*

Nature put its own barrier, the green Purbeck Hills, between Creech and Tyneham but in our own century man added a much greater one and called it the National Interest. It was the nation's Christmas present to Tyneham and district in 1943. On December 19 the last inhabitants moved out and the tanks rolled in, using ten square miles for shooting practice. "The Government appreciate that this is no small sacrifice which you are asked to make but they are sure that you will give this further help towards winning the war with a good heart," said the eviction notice.

The villagers left believing that they would return when the war was over. "Please treat the church and houses with care," said the touching note which they left pinned on the door of Tyneham church. "We have given up our homes, where many of us have lived for generations, to help win the war and to keep men free. We shall return one day and thank you for treating the village kindly."

But they never did return and while sympathisers campaigned for the Government to honour its pledge, the village was reduced to ruin by shellfire and neglect. For those with roots in Tyneham, the wind blown in by the guns of the Lulworth Ranges was an ill one indeed, yet few winds offer profit to no-one and this was no exception. The greatest beneficiaries were the wildlife for whom the threat from shellfire was infinitely smaller than the destructive side-effects of intensive farming and unrestricted public access. "Thanks to the army, Tyneham has become the greatest natural wilderness on this side of Dartmoor, which makes it unique in lowland England," says Rodney Legg, once the most vociferous campaigner for the displaced human population.

There is more, for Tyneham has a long history and the absence of modern machines has been the salvation of medieval field systems and the remains of Saxon banks and hedges. Also preserved is a strange ghost-town atmosphere, the result of decades without the creeping accessories of life in the twentieth century. The cottages in Post Office Row are now in skeletal form but the church and schoolroom survive and the antique telephone box is restored, to be admired by the curious since Tyneham was reopened to the public on days when the guns are silent.

Tyneham... lost to the "national interest". The early telephone box has since been restored.

Towards East Creech in Purbeck

CORFE CASTLE AND ITS VILLAGE

It was inevitable that Corfe would have a castle for its peculiar geography makes it an obvious fortress location. Standing on a natural, steep-sided hillock a few miles inland, it is perfectly placed to guard the only cleft in the twelve-mile ridge of the Purbeck Hills. The Saxons probably recognised its strategic value for there was a building of substance here long before the Norman Conquest. Traditionally the site is associated with the cold-blooded killing in 978 of the sainted King Edward the Martyr, a victim of his step-mother's ruthless ambition for her own son.

William I began the royal castle whose ruins we know

Corfe village... many shops and houses are built of stone from the castle ruins

today, described by the Royal Commission on Historical Monuments as "one of the most important buildings in the country". It was extended and strengthened several times and remained in royal hands for 200 years, serving as palace and prison, fortress and bank vault. The Conqueror's eldest son, Robert Duke of Normandy, was imprisoned there in 1106 and King Edward II 220 years later. King John made it a favourite haunt, storing treasures in the castle and staying there during his extended hunting trips to Purbeck's royal forest.

Fortress Corfe tasted military action in 1138 when a rebellious Baron de Redvers resisted a siege during the troubled reign of King Stephen. It tasted it in a bigger way during the English Civil War, holding out for almost three years against Parliamentary forces until finally betrayed in 1646 by an officer of the Royalist garrison. Soon after one of England's earliest and greatest Norman castles was blown apart by order of the House of Commons.

Since 1981 Corfe Castle has belonged to the National Trust, bequeathed as part of an historic 16,000-acre estate by the Honourable Ralph Bankes, descendant of the heroic Lady Bankes, who led the remarkable defence of the building from 1643-46. Even in ruins it remains an imposing structure, dominating the landscape from either side of "the gap at Corfe", as the Anglo-Saxon Chronicle describes it. Below are the quaintly attractive buildings of Corfe village, its character little changed since Treves called it "a wrinkled old place in the winter of its age, lying at the foot of its Castle like a faithful hound", its three little streets leading "humbly to the Castle gate".

An autumn dawn at Corfe Castle

OLD HARRY AND ANVIL POINT

One of the old names for Swanage is Sandwich, which is oddly appropriate, for the erosion-prone wealden foundations of its valley form the meat of a geological sandwich. To the south is a chunky slice of limestone, providing quarrymen with their product and mariners with a sheer wall of hard stone from St Alban's Head to Anvil Point; to the north is a thin sliver of chalk, tenuously linked to the great chalk mass of north and central Dorset and meeting its admiring public at Old Harry Rocks.

Poor Harry himself is a widower today for his wife collapsed in a gale and sank beneath the waves almost 100 years ago. It's said he went into mourning then, aided by Victorian fishermen who painted a black band around him. Old Harry is and his wife was a sea-stack detached from the main chalk cliffs by the action of the sea. Someday he'll follow the route to a watery grave, for the cliffs here are retreating. In the meantime other stacks are being created, the largest in 1921 when the sea broke through a narrow wall of chalk and created St Lucas Leap. Chalk arches have also appeared, and then there is the smuggler's cave called Parson's Barn.

"There is humour in these names," Purbeck's principal historian Rodney Legg tells us. "Parson's Barn, for instance, took its name because there is a proverbial saying in Dorset that no barn is more accommodating than a parson's, and the vast space in that lofty cave offered the ultimate in barns. St Lucas Leap has its saintly name borrowed from, believe it or not, a pedigree greyhound that is said to have dropped over the cliff there whilst coursing a hare!" Old Harry himself is the devil in disguise and the clifftop nearby is called Old Nick's Ground.

The lighthouse at Anvil Point

South of Swanage, and beyond the Durlston Country Park with its informative castle walls and famous globe of stone, the lighthouse of Anvil Point flashes out its nightly warning, as it has since 1881. Nearby are the Tilly Whim Caves, a retired quarry given a second career by the smugglers of the nineteenth century and a third by the tourists of the twentieth.

*Old Harry and
Handfast Point*

NATURE AND INDUSTRY AT ARNE AND WAREHAM

The story of the ragged south and west shores of Poole Harbour is a tale of wildlife and industry living side by side. Today the Dartford warbler shares its heathland habitat with the twentieth century technology of British Petroleum but the pattern was established long ago. When the Romans arrived in the first century AD they found Iron Age settlements here and an active pottery industry. Using the local clay, potters made thin-walled pots which did not shrink when fired and were ideal for cooking. The pottery impressed the Romans and soon the native people of these quiet harbour shores were sending their black burnished ware to the whole of Roman Britain.

Recent archaeology on the BP pipeline yielded evidence of a 50-acre Romano-British site at Cleavel Point; nearby is evidence of medieval activity 1,000 years later. South of Ower Farm, pits created by clay extraction for twelfth century pottery had been backfilled with tons of seashells – evidence, say archaeologists, of what amounted to a "medieval seafood pickling factory"!

Clay extraction resumed in the late seventeenth century, expanded in the eighteenth, when the prized product was transported to the Staffordshire Potteries and elsewhere, and has continued on a grand scale to the present. Today, though, Purbeck's ball clay is upstaged by the liquid gold which has made Wytch Farm the biggest onshore oilfield in Europe. Together these two great industries, one rooted in the distant past, the other of recent origin, sit uneasily in an area of great environmental sensitivity. They are almost surrounded by nature reserves and sites of special interest, including four of national importance. The Arne peninsula alone has the nine-acre national reserve of Big

Wood, where salt marsh transforms into woodland, and 1,000 acres owned by the Royal Society for the Protection of Birds. Here is the British headquarters of the Dartford warbler, a shy and secretive creature, popular with the common-or-garden birdwatcher. The bird's problems are its dependence on the diminishing heathland and its vulnerability to the harshest of British winters. Its numbers dropped to ten pairs in 1962-63 but multiplied to a three-figure Dorset count in the milder 1980s.

Ball clay mine and Wareham from Whiteway Hill

The Arne Peninsula, looking south-east

According to Henry VIII's travelling topographer John Leland, "there lie three isles in the haven of Poole, the most famous of which is Brunkeshey". He was right about Brownsea but wrong about the number of islands. There are eight with names and writer Richard Blomfield counted even more by including "various small islets" in 1984.

Brownsea is the biggest island, being one-and-a-half miles long and three-quarters-of-a-mile across, and is the only one which can be readily visited by the public. Others of substance include Furzey and Green Islands south-west of Brownsea, Long and Round Islands east of Arne, Pergins Island in Holes Bay and Gigger's Island in the mouth of the Wareham river. Long and Round Islands come close to being united at low water when a strip of marshland between them is largely exposed. Round Island covers fifteen acres and provides a spectacular display of purple rhododendrons in spring and of golden gorse and white broom later.

It was inevitable that there would be a port in Poole Harbour but the original port was not at Poole but Wareham. But for the subtleties of harbour geography we might now speak not Wareham Harbour rather than Poole.

Wareham – sandwiched between the Rivers Frome and Piddle – has an ancient history with settlements traceable back to the late Iron Age. Claims of a strong Roman connection are dubious but the Saxons left evidence in plenty, including defensive banks on three sides, built in King Alfred's time, when the threat of Viking raids was at its height. The Danes captured Wareham several times and whiled away a winter there in 876.

The River Frome at Wareham

The Danish interest probably reflects Wareham's high standing as a Saxon trading port and military base. It remained a port until the fourteenth century, when larger ships and the silting of the Frome and Wareham Channel gave its new rival across the harbour a decisive advantage. Thereafter Wareham's importance declined, except during the English Civil War, when its proximity to the royalist stronghold of Corfe Castle briefly renewed its strategic importance. Like Beaminster, Dorcester Blandford and Sturminster Newton, it also suffered a great fire disaster which destroyed much of the town in 1762.

Round Island from Arne

65

POOLE HARBOUR FROM CORFE AND SANDBANKS

With its assortment of islands and islets, its silted shallows broken by deeper channels, its peninsulas, inlets, bays and inner havens, Poole Harbour offers an almost archipelago-type environment. It's said to be the world's second largest natural harbour, boasting twenty-eight square miles of water and ninety miles of muddy coastline. Through a fluke of geography, it benefits from four high tides a day, the result of tidal interference by the Isle of Wight, which forces each twice-daily surge into partial retreat to give Poole a second flood-tide three hours after the first.

In modern times Poole Harbour's shallowness (the average depth is a mere two feet) has been its greatest commercial handicap, causing the automatic exclusion of the great liners and tankers of the twentieth century. But shipping's loss has been wildlife's gain for birds especially continue to thrive along the harbour and island shores.

Until Victorian times, urban Poole was largely confined to the peninsula which the High Street still bisects. "It standeth almost as an isle in its haven," John Leland observed in about 1540. Of Brownsea, the largest genuine isle in the haven, he wrote: "Some say that there has been a parish in it. There is yet a chapel for an hermit. It 'longeth to Cerne Abbey. The chapel was dedicated to St Andrew, of which and the hermitage, there are no remains."

Fifteen centuries before Leland's time, the Romans passed this way, a few settling on Brownsea but most sailing on to Hamworthy to take the road to Wimborne and the north. But it was Henry VIII who made best use of the island's obvious

Sunset over Brownsea, from Shore Road, Poole

strategic value, building a blockhouse in 1547 to guard the harbour entrance. Brownsea was used for copperas production in the seventeenth century and acquired a greater castle and grounds in the eighteenth. But its greatest claims to fame are of the twentieth for it hosted Baden-Powell's first scout camp in 1907 and, as a National Trust property, today provides not only a nature reserve but a rare southern outpost for that retreating native of British woodland, the red squirrel.

Towards Poole Harbour from West Hill, Corfe

EVENING VIEWS AT POOLE

Poole is known for the beauty of its sunsets, admired by generations of men and women who have paused to admire the evening views across the harbour. Long before photographs were invented, the great J. M. W. Turner came here and was inspired to paint the harbour at sunset from Evening Hill. Was it called Evening Hill because of the views it offers as the sun goes down? It is tempting to think so.

Poole and its harbour have been known for much more in their time, including the notorious pirate Harry Pay. The Spanish called him "Arripay", a seagoing knight who "scours the seas as

Evening Light on Sandbanks, from Evening Hill

a corsair, with many ships, plundering all the Spanish and French vessels that he could meet with". Eventually the continentals sought revenge, sailing into medieval Poole at dawn and causing widespread death and destruction. Pay's brother was among those killed but Harry himself was away on pirates' business and survived.

The smuggling era brought more drama and a famous incident in 1747, when smugglers broke into the Customs warehouse on the Quay and took back their cargo of tea. "We come for our own and will have it," they told the nightwatchman after tying him up.

Poole's commercial heyday was the eighteenth and early nineteenth centuries when North Atlantic fish made Dorset merchants rich. The fleets left Poole in spring with supplies for the cod-based colonies in Newfoundland; they dried their catch and sold it in the West Indies or Mediterranean, then brought West Indian or Mediterranean goods to England. But in the nineteenth century the cod trade collapsed, causing an economic slump in Poole and even greater hardship in Newfoundland.

Poole's fortunes revived a century ago and remain bouyant as the town reaps once again the benefits of its great natural harbour. In the evenings, at weekends and throughout the summer season the Quay comes alive, though today tourists, diners and drinkers outnumber those concerned with the commercial work of the port. On the water pleasure craft of every description mingle in great numbers with the truck ferries, cargo ships and fishing boats which ply the deepwater channels as their predecessors did for centuries in the age of sail.

Digging for bait at sunset in Poole Harbour

BOURNEMOUTH: BEACH AND TOWN

In 180 years, Bournemouth has raced from a late and standing start to become the biggest and richest town in Dorset, filling with bricks and tarmac the wildnerness which once separated the historic towns of Poole and Christchurch. Two centuries ago Bournemouth was neither in Dorset nor a town; it was not even a village. Smugglers were the commonest visitors then, dropping anchor in the bay and rowing or wading ashore with great cargoes of wine and spirits, tea and tobacco. The smooth, deserted beaches and wild, uninhabited heathland beyond made this ideal smuggling country; each year an estimated 80,000 gallons of brandy alone were carted along the sandy tracks which today form the artery roads of a modern seaside town.

When the nineteenth century dawned there was only one house in what is now central Bournemouth. It was called the Decoy Pond House, taking its name from a wildfowlers' duck pool near the site of today's Bournemouth Square. Then came Captain and Mrs Lewis Tregonwell, the gentle folk from Cranborne who built a seaside retreat overlooking the break in the cliffs where the humble Bourne Stream met the breaking waves of the English Channel. Others followed; by the middle of the century a substantial village had appeared; by the turn of the century Bournemouth was a town of county borough status, a fashionable Victorian resort whose claims of cure by climate attracted the unhealthy and wealthy alike.

The population increased tenfold between 1870 and 1900 and has more than doubled again since then. Highways, housing estates and modern office blocks have appeared where once were carpets of grass or gorse and heather. Some represent a second

Modern office blocks at St Paul's Place, Bournemouth

generation of development, replacing the Victorian villas built a century or so ago. On the outskirts, the historic villages of Kinson, Iford, Wick, Throop and Holdenhurst, which once perched on the fringe of a great heath, now find themselves absorbed into an even greater conurbation.

Bournemouth – transferred from Hampshire to Dorset in 1974 – is often called a town without history, yet it has packed much into its 180 years, attracting great names from royalty and politics, art and literature, stage and screen. Today it has largely shed its bathchair image of the past and matured into a modern seaside and conference town and a significant centre for trade and finance.

Bournemouth from Hengistbury Head

CHRISTCHURCH AND HENGISTBURY FROM STANPIT

The Saxon name for Christchurch was Twynham, meaning the place between two rivers. These are the Dorset Stour and Hampshire Avon, whose waters meet in Christchurch Harbour where they also reach the sea. Like Bournemouth, this was Hampshire territory until 1974, which meant, oddly, that the Dorset Stour neither started nor ended its journey in Dorset. Today the Hampshire Avon is the river of greater confusion for it, like the Stour, begins in Wiltshire and meets the sea in Dorset.

Christchurch is a town steeped in history from every age. Evidence of ancient British interest comes through barrows and earthworks; the invading Romans had a camp of some sort here and the Saxons built defences to fend off Danish raiders. The Normans, inevitably, built a castle whose remains survive; they also left a solid dwelling, the Constable's House, now a roofless ruin but a rare survivor of its age. But the jewel the Christchurch crown, dwarfing all around it, is the Priory Church, the longest parish church in England.

According to tradition, the church was originally to be built on St Catherine's Hill outside the present town. But whatever was built there by day was mysteriously dismantled at night and transported to a new site a mile to the south. This happened several times and at last the builders took the hint and followed their materials. On the alternative plot a model workman joined them, labouring hard all day but never appearing at mealtimes or to draw his pay. One day a great beam was found to be a foot too short. The unknown workman placed his hand upon it and instantly it fitted. With this he disappeared and was never seen again. But the church was named after him – Christchurch – and the beam survives.

The greatest natural landmark hereabouts is the crumbling promontory of Hengistbury Head, which protects much of Christchurch and its harbour from the sea yet struggles to protect itself. Ten thousand years ago this was an inland hilltop and the home of Stone Age hunters. You could walk to the Isle of Wight from here, though the sea's intentions were clear. The waves need no assistance in their erosive work but they obtained some from a Victorian mining company which removed vast slices of the headland to extract its iron ore.

Hengistbury Head from Stanpit

Christchurch from Stanpit

MUDEFORD AND CHRISTCHURCH HARBOUR

Mudeford is an odd little place, "marred by modern development", as Jo Draper says, yet able to fill its spacious car parks on any sunny Sunday or public holiday. Despite the modern development, Mudeford Quay itself retains a fishing village atmosphere, with boats, tackle and lobster pots always in evidence and a clutch of buildings which have changed little in 200 years. Nearby powerful currents sweep through the harbour mouth, their route often changing under the influence of wind and tide. The channel is known as the Run; nearby is the notorious Christchurch Ledge, providing regular work for the lifeboat crew whose boathouse stands on the Quay.

In 1784 this sea-swept spit witnessed a scene of great drama as smugglers did battle with the men of His Majesty's Navy. The smugglers were protecting a huge cargo involving 120,000 gallons of spirits and twenty-five tons of tea. Three hundred men were employed to land and carry away the goods, with 400 horses and fifty wagons. The Navy and Customs intervened and were met by a volley of shots which killed one officer and wounded several men. The battle lasted three hours but the contraband was gotten safely away.

Mudeford was honoured with a royal visit in 1803 when George III stopped off on his way by sea to Weymouth. The Scots Greys, the Yeomanry and the Christchurch Volunteers all turned out to fire salutes from the shore. "After that Mudeford brightened and increased the number of its bathing machines," says Arthur Mee.

It was a long time before Mudeford Quay – otherwise known as the Haven – was brightened. As one Victorian visitor

Lobster pots on Mudeford Quay

from Wimborne noted in 1892: "The Haven consisted of two or three tumbledown Irish-looking houses on a narrow, sandy, flat peninsula with a bit of strap grass in the centre, sporting a few stunted pine trees and scraggy furze, surrounded by that diabolical invention barbed wire." Happily, Mudeford has put its quay in order since then, with a solid seawall, lined and metalled car park, cafeteria and shops.

Mudeford from Hengistbury Head

WIMBORNE AND THE STOUR AT PAMPHILL

Visitors today find Wimborne an appealing old town, undeserving of the caustic comments which Sir Frederick Treves heaped upon it eighty-five years ago. Treves saved the sharpest weapons from his extensive armoury of insults for Wimborne, describing it as commonplace, characterless and "successfully mediocre". "It looks its best when seen from a distance," he added, drily.

Wimborne has a long history for the area was well-populated in prehistoric times and reluctantly hosted part of the Roman invasion following the choice of Lake Gates as the base camp of Vespasian's conquering Second Legion in AD 43. The Wimborne by-pass now crosses part of the site.

Like Treves' insults, Wimborne's virtues tend to come in twos and threes. It has two towers on its Minster, one of the late Norman period, the other of the fifteenth century; it has two rivers, the Stour and the Allen, or three if we count the millstream which breaks from the Allen for its passage through the town centre; it has three fine stone bridges, Julians and Walford from the seventeenth century, Canford from the early nineteenth.

Wimborne has many fine buildings, among them the Priest's House Museum, built in the sixteenth, seventeenth and eighteenth centuries and now authentically restored with its exquisite bow windows last seen 100 years ago. Nearby is the jewel in the Wimborne crown, the magnificent Minster church, dedicated to its founder St Cuthburga, who was abbess here almost 1,300 years ago. The town did things in duplicate even then for it had both a monastery and a nunnery.

The Minster (which even Treves is forced to compliment as

Pamphill from Eye Footbridge

"gracious") dates mostly from the twelfth to fifteenth centuries and has a mottled complexion through its unusual mix of grey and red stone. It holds much of interest for the visitor, including its fourteenth century astronomical clock, its chained library where Matthew Prior the poet studied, its timekeeping grenadier, the Quarterjack, who strikes every fifteen minutes from his post high on the west tower. Then there is the eccentric Anthony Ettricke's tomb, set in the wall in accordance with his wish to be buried neither within the Minster nor outside it. He died in 1703 but the date on the chest has been unsubtly altered from 1693 – the year he wrongly predicted for his death!

Wimborne Minster from the south-west, in winter

THE STOUR AT STURMINSTER MARSHALL

It stands today as it has stood for centuries, solid and steadfast, immovable and largely unmoved by the passing Stour or the passing world. It is arguably the most beautiful bridge in Dorset, probably the oldest and certainly the finest of Norman construction. Some date it from the fourteenth century, others from the twelfth. It may have been built around 1175, forty years before King John put his name to Magna Charta.

Its name is White Mill Bridge, though it is many years since a millstone turned in its vicinity. Its eight arches span the Stour near Sturminster Marshall, carrying the road which may once have been the main route between Dorchester and Wimborne. If so, then it probably lost its principal function in life when construction of Julians Bridge provided a more direct way into Wimborne in 1636. The change has proved its salvation,

The Stour at Sturminster Marshall

enabling it to remain close to its original form instead of being widened for the twentieth century.

Not that it is completely unscathed for traction engines began to widen its width until banned from the bridge in 1909. They were fortunate for the bridge threatens transportation for life to any human causing damage, though the present plaque is a replacement for the original, stolen in 1988.

Like a more famous Norman structure, Winchester Cathedral, the bridge was built on wooden foundations, its heavy stone buttresses supported by rafts of oak and those in turn by oak piles sunk into the riverbed. Bridge engineers uncovered the foundations after flood damage in 1964. The rafts were replaced by concrete then but the piles – perfectly preserved for eight centuries by the absence of oxygen – were allowed to remain.

White Mill Bridge has had many admirers, including Monica Hutchings, who paused here on her journey up the Stour in the '50s and heard the legend of Knowlton bells. It happened long ago, when Knowlton church, near Cranborne, was disused but not yet ruined. To the people of Sturminster Marshall, it seemed the answer to a prayer, for their church needed bells and Knowlton had them. One dark night they crept across the downs and claimed their prize. But the loss was soon discovered and as the bell-stealers neared their own village they heard the Knowltonians gaining ground behind them. In their panic they tipped the bells into the river near White Mill Bridge, intending to retrieve them later. They tried, more than once, but the bells always slipped back.

White Mill Bridge, Sturminster Marshall

TOWERS AT HORTON AND ST GILES

Neighbours as well as cousins in the fraternity of follies are Horton Tower and the Philosopher's Tower, two eccentric products of the eighteenth century village squires whose descendants still preside over the country estates north of Wimborne. But that is where the similarity ends for they are contrastingly different in scale, impact and design.

The Philosopher's Tower, near Wimborne St Giles

Horton Tower is tall and dominant and its six storeys, built of brick on a hilltop, provide a well-known landmark visible from much of East Dorset. Newman and Pevsner call it a "meglomaniac folly", naming Humphry Sturt of Horton as its probable creator. "His folie de grandeur found further expression after 1765 when he moved across to More Crichel."

Sturt's purpose is not entirely clear. His tower may have been a folly for its own sake, or an astronomical observatory as suggested in 1765, or a smugglers' lookout tower as alleged in the present century. In later life, when age and infirmity prevented him from riding with hounds, Sturt is said to have watched the hunt's progress from his hexagonal turreted tower.

In the middle of the present century it was still possible to enjoy the view from the top of the tower but the roof, floors and steps are now all gone. It has already achieved a measure of immortality, however, as the scene of cockfighting in the film of Hardy's Far From the Madding Crowd and now appears fair set for a future as a telecommunications tower.

Unlike Horton Tower, the Philosopher's is short and squat and, on its sloping greenfield sight, visible only to travellers on the road from Wimborne to Cranborne. It has two storeys, a domed roof and walls of brick. It was built as a place for contemplation by the third Earl of Shaftesbury, known as the "Philosopher Earl". "Presumably he wished to copy the example of the great French philosopher Montaigne, who first set the fashion for philosophers to live in a tower," says Osborn.

Horton Tower from Sovell Down, above Gussage All Saints

CHURCHES AT CHALBURY AND KNOWLTON

One stands on a hilltop, complete and cared for, with white-washed walls and a distinctive eighteenth century appearance; the other, an abandoned Norman ruin, squats soberly within a circular earthwork, its tower and walls of flint broken and roofless, reduced to the role of picnic site and object of curiosity. Such are the contrasts between the churches of Chalbury and Knowlton, neighbours in the geographical sense but with features and fortunes that are miles apart.

Surprisingly, All Saints, Chalbury, is only a little younger than Knowlton church for it was built in the thirteenth century. It owes its present appearance to extensive rebuilding and remodelling in the eighteenth century and wall rendering in the twentieth, which has hidden the original walls of rubble and flint.

The church stands on Chalbury Hill, 300 feet at its summit and overlooking much of Dorset and Hampshire. Its height has ensured Chalbury a special role in the community, storing water in its hilltop reservoir today, sending signals from a telegraph station two centuries ago. In 1805 news of victory at Trafalgar passed this way, signalled by shutters along a line of hills from Plymouth to London.

Chalbury's known history is mostly modern but Knowlton made its greatest contributions before records began. It must have been a place of substance then for the trappings of prehistoric life can be found all around. The church itself is within the rings of a henge; there are two similar henges nearby and Bronze Age barrows abound.

Knowlton was still important in Norman times, named as

Knowlton ruins at sundown

a royal manor in the Domesday Book and an administrative hundred in 1332. A fair was held in the medieval village, which occupied 400 yards along the south bank of the Allen. We might be tempted to surmise that the village fell victim to the fourteenth century Black Death, yet the same century brought extensions to the church, suggesting Knowlton was growing rather than dying. For some reason, though, the village did die. The church was temporarily abandoned around 1650, repaired in the eighteenth century, then abandoned for good soon after when its roof fell in.

*Chalbury church on
a frosty morning*

CRANBORNE CHASE AND MANOR

In history as well as in name, Cranborne Chase and Cranborne Manor are inextricably linked. The Chase, from the eleventh century to the nineteenth, was one of the great hunting grounds of England, a forest playground where kings and nobles came for sport, where the interests of deer were second only to those of the men who came to hunt them. The Manor was the official centre of the medieval Chase, a hunting lodge built for King John in 1208, a place where offenders against forest laws could be tried and perhaps imprisoned.

Some parts of the present house survive from King John's time but most of the building was the creation of Robert Cecil, first Earl of Salisbury, whose descendants still own it. He was chief minister to Elizabeth I, who sold him the Manor, and James I, in whose reign he transformed it.

Long before Salisbury's time, or even King John's, Cranborne Chase was earning its place in history and in pre-history. Neolithic man left evidence in plenty of his ritualistic lifestyle, including the dramatic Dorset cursus, two parallel ditches and banks 100 yards apart, six miles long and aligned to the midwinter sunset. From the Bronze Age the evidence is of a struggle for survival as the climate cooled and the chalkland soil became increasingly eroded. Iron Age inhabitants were better equipped and better organised but not to the extent of the Romans, whose Ackling Dyke crosses the downs on its way between Exeter and London.

Close to the Roman Road are the villages of Woodyates, where the poet Robert Browning's ancestors lived, and Pentridge, Hardy's Tantridge, where Tess came in search of an aristocratic

Cranborne Manor and its beech avenue in winter

kinsman and, later, to tend Mrs Stoke-d'Urberville's fowls. Pentridge remains one of civilization's backwaters, little changed since Treves called it a "dim retreat" which offered "such peace and seclusion as even the cloisters of a convent may lack".

Turning his flak on Cranborne, Treves wrote of "a straggling, absent-minded little place" with "apparently small purpose in life". Once its purposes were great and manyfold, for it was an important administrative centre with a Saxon abbey as well as a royal hunting lodge. But it was destined to be overlooked in turn by the canal age, the turnpikes and the railways and has been backpeddling ever since.

Towards Cranborne Chase

FONTMELL MAGNA AND ASHMORE

Once every ten years pilgrims gather on the hills of Cranborne Chase for a ceremony whose origins are rooted in seventeenth century history. Drawn by a sense of tradition and respect for the courage and devotion of their forbears, they assemble on the hills above Ashgrove and journey down to a Quaker burial ground hidden in a deep valley called Chevicombe Bottom. The cemetery was provided by William Fry of Higher Ashgrove Farm soon after his conversion to Quakerism in 1657. Quakers were persecuted then and denied the right to burial in consecrated ground. Fry stipulated that Quakers should have "free liberty to come to and from the burying place by the way now used" and the ten-yearly ceremony ensures that their rights are maintained.

Ashmore, the highest village in Dorset

Ashmore has a long tradition of Quakerism and founder himself, George Fox, attended an illegal meeting in Fry's house in 1663. In the eighteenth century Ashmore estate and village were bought by a Quaker and merchant from London, John Eliot, who closed both village pubs and opened a school.

It was not only Quakers who sought sanctuary on Cranborne Chase for this was, as Treves said, a "rough, mysterious country", and it attracted many rough and mysterious people. It was a forest wildnerness, a perfect refuge for those needing an escape route from society. Poachers lived on the Chase in great numbers, smugglers too, along with thieves, murderers and rogues of every kind. These desperate inhabitants did little to enhance the reputation of the historic hunting forest; the deer did even less. Estimates of their number ranged in the early nineteenth century from 5,000 to 20,000; they roamed, freely and with legal protection, across 7,000 acres of woodland, 10,000 acres of commons and sheep walks, 15,000 acres of arable. They were the cause of crop damage on a grand scale, of violence between poacher and gamekeeper, of legal disputes between one neighbour and another, of a great public debate which rumbled on for years.

At length the Chase had, as Treves puts it, to be "put down as a mere covert for wickedness". In 1830 an Act of Parliament severed the rights of the Chase at their roots; the woodman's axe took over, the farmer's plough came close behind; swiftly and efficiently, the forest habitat was destroyed, and with it most of the deer which had sheltered there for 700 years.

Fontmell Down, near Shaftesbury, now a nature reserve

SPRING AND AUTUMN NEAR SHAFTESBURY

Within three miles of the well-worn cobbles of Shaftesbury's Gold Hill, the most famous street in Dorset, is a rural road which states its own case for recognition. It will never be a location for Hovis commercials but the road up Zigzag Hill to Charlton Down is a route once driven, never forgotten. From a valley north of Melbury Abbas, it takes the traveller by a series of hairpins to the very roof of Dorset. At its summit Dorset meets Wiltshire and the eye meets the landscape of Cranborne Chase. Close by is Win Green, 910 feet above sea level and the Chase's highest point. Only Wiltshire and Pilsdon Pen are glad that it is not in Dorset.

The Chase is a landscape of open chalk ridges and steeply dipping vales, punctuated here and there by clumps of woodland, survivors from the days when this was a great hunting forest. As Desmond Hawkins says, it was possible then to ride from Southampton to Bath without deviating often or greatly from forest or chase.

Thomas Hardy appreciated the primitive character of Cranborne Chase before its deforestation, a "truly venerable tract of forest land, one of the few remaining woodlands in England of undoubted primeval date, wherein Druidical mistletoe was still found on aged oaks, and where enormous yew-trees, not planted by the hand of man, grew as they had grown when they were pollarded for bows". Virginia Woolf, a visitor in 1926, observed "the stunted aboriginal forest trees, scattered, not grouped in cultivations; anemones, bluebells, violets, all pale, sprinkled about, without colour ... for the sun hardly shone".

Sir Frederick Treves wrote of the Chase's "rolling woodland, backed by white clouds in an azure sky", of a blue mist which "hangs in the winding glens like the smoke of incense", of patches of ploughed land on the forest outskirts, almost rust red in colour, together with "light green stretches of springing corn and clumps of dark pines", fringed by white may blossom and yellow gorse. To these colours he added the paler yellow of primroses splashed on the banks of a trackway, the blue of bluebells "so closely clustered that they look in the shade like a deep, blue pool". Between the primroses and the bluebells were white anemones and "violets beyond number".

Beech woods at Zigzag Hill in autumn

Woods in spring on the Rushmore Estate, near Shaftesbury

BLANDFORD VIEW AND HINTON ST MARY MILL

Blandford Forum is the self-professed Phoenix of Dorset, rising from the ashes of a great and disastrous fire to become a model Georgian town. Other Dorset towns suffered greatly from fires and all were rebuilt, but none offers quite the same architectural impact as Blandford. Jo Draper calls it "the best, most complete, small Georgian town in England"; Newman and Pevsner see it as one of the nation's "most satisfying Georgian ensembles".

For these and other favourable reviews, Blandford owes almost everything to two brothers, the architects and builders John and William Bastard. They had a business in the town in 1731, the year in which the great fire, caused by sparks from a chimney setting light to a thatched roof, destroyed three-quarters of a town described by Defoe a few years earlier as "handsome and well-built". It was an immense tragedy, costing at least fourteen lives and making 480 homeless, but it also gave the Bastard brothers, as official surveyors, a rare opportunity to plan and build a town virtually from scratch.

The reconstruction around and beyond the spacious Market Place took about thirty years. The Bastards themselves built the church, the town hall and many other buildings; they also influenced the design of buildings for which they were not directly responsible. As a result there is, as Newman and Pevsner put it, "a distinct architectural flavour about the whole, the basic uniformity of design and materials being relieved just enough by spirited individual touches".

Blandford Forum is a town born of the River Stour; its very name suggests a market near a ford, as did its other medieval name, Cheping Blaneford. Here centuries ago was an important crossing point.

Twelve miles away, beyond another town of the Stour, Sturminster Newton, is Hinton St Mary, which made its own contribution to history in 1963, when a fine Roman mosaic pavement was discovered in its midst. It features the head of Christ and found a new home at the British Museum. Like most riverside communities, Hinton formerly had its own flour mill, known as Cutt or Cutt's Mill. Its wheel and machinery were already redundant when Monica Hutchings rested here during her journey up the Stour in 1956; they remain so, unlike those of its neighbour at Sturminster, now working once again.

Redundant mill-wheel, Cutt's Mill, Hinton St Mary

Blandford Forum from Langton meadows

BULBARROW AND THE BRIDGE AT FIFEHEAD NEVILLE

At 902 feet, Bulbarrow is second only to Pilsdon Pen in the hierarchy of Dorset hills, and its views are second to none. To the north-west the Somerset Quantocks can be seen on the clearest days, to the north-east the Saxon town of Shaftesbury, to the south-east the hills of mid-Hampshire, to the south-west the memorial to Nelson's Hardy on its hill above Portesham. To the eighteenth century historian John Hutchins, it was a view which "surpasses all imagination"; Treves described a "waving valley of green fields, with trees in lines, in knolls, in avenues, in dots; a red roof, the glitter of a trout stream, the trail of a white road, and at the end blue-grey hills so far away that they seem to be made of a sea mist".

The patchwork stretching away from Bulbarrow's northern and western foothills is the Blackmore Vale, the largest and most famous valley in Dorset. Centuries ago it was a hunting forest – the Forest of the White Hart – but today it is one of the leading dairying areas of Britain. Thomas Hardy described the Vale at length in Tess of the d'Urbervilles, calling it an "engirdled and secluded region, for the most part untrodden as yet by tourist or landscape painter". Hardy believed that the Vale was best viewed from the hill summits around it. He contrasts it with the "calcereous downs and cornlands" to the south. "Here, in the valley, the world seems to be constructed upon a smaller and more delicate scale; the fields are mere paddocks, so reduced that from this height their hedgerows appear a network of dark green threads overspreading the pale green of the grass."

The Blackmore Vale is veined by streams and brooks which feed the River Stour, among them the Divelish, spanned near Fifehead Neville by a picturesque packhorse bridge, a medieval structure and a scheduled ancient monument. Its railings are a relatively modern acquisition for it was originally built with low parapets and no rails to avoid contact with the sidepacks of the animals which used it. Wallis says the straight-sided arches are unusual and would constitute a weakness if the bridge had to carry heavy loads. It doesn't, because today's traffic uses the adjacent "Irish" bridge, a ford with pipes beneath it which carry some of the water, or all of it in dry weather.

The packhorse bridge and River Divelish, Fifehead Neville

Looking west from Bulbarrow Hill

These days sheep are outnumbered by cattle in Dorset but it was not always so. In fact the county was once famous for its flocks, whose number and size caught every traveller's eye. "It is believed that no place in England affordeth more sheep in so small a compass as this county," the clergyman Thomas Fuller noted in 1661. Sixty years later Daniel Defoe was sceptical when told that 600,000 sheep grazed the downs around Dorchester: "but when I viewed the country round, I confess I could not but incline to believe it".

Like its sheep, Minterne Magna is a creature of the chalk downs. It sits in hilly, wooded country, offering fine inland views from its hilltops. Thomas Hardy called it Great Hintock and in his time it acquired a new manor house, built on Elizabethan foundations for Lord Digby in 1903-6. It remains the Digby seat.

The same family provides the link between Minterne Magna and Sherborne, North Dorset's biggest town. The Digbys bought Sherborne Castle in 1616, soon after the execution of the previous owner, Sir Walter Raleigh. A story is told of an occasion when tobacco's first importer was enjoying a smoke in his grounds and was suddenly doused by a bucket of ale thrown by a servant who thought he was on fire!

The twelfth century Old Castle is now a ruin, destroyed after two Civil War sieges, the second led by Cromwell himself, who called it a "malicious, mischievous castle, like its owner". The "New" Castle, begun by Raleigh and extended by the Digbys, stands nearby.

Few Dorset places are more attractive than Sherborne, few more steeped in history. It was a cathedral town in Saxon times, founded by St Aldhelm, its first bishop, in 705 but losing its status to Old Sarum 370 years later. The cathedral by then was a monastic abbey church, which it remained until 1539. Only fragments of the Anglo-Saxon church survive (features which are "minor but important", say Newman and Pevsner) and most of the present Sherborne Abbey is fifteenth century. Its features include fan vaulting of that era, said by some to be the finest in England. The abbey is the great architectural treasure of Sherborne and one of the greatest treasures of Dorset.

Limes and an ornate Digby memorial in Sherborne Abbey churchyard

*Sheep in the snow at
Minterne Magna*

INDEX OF PLACENAMES

Gold Hill, Shaftesbury... the most photographed street in Dorset?